Born in the 1950s to a submariner and a 'cockney' rebel, he engaged early with sport and books. A deep thirst for knowledge was well served by King Edward IV Grammar and the University of London. Playing a respectable level of football, golf and with a thirty-five-year squash habit, it became apparent that he'd need to work for a living. After a season at Butlin's, cost accounting, grass-cutting for the RAF, and an accidental gap year, he stumbled into brewing. Thirty-five years later, after running sales teams across the UK, he set up his own business. An ensuing sense of freedom drew him back to creative writing.

Janette
Sean & Francesca
Michael, Liz, Rhys, Ethan, Esme & Lucas,
Anthony, Guayarmina, Eloisa & Mateo

Kevin Paul Mellor

RAMBLINGS OF A
FREE MAN

Join me on my Journey

[signature] A Mc 2025

AUSTIN MACAULEY PUBLISHERS®

LONDON • CAMBRIDGE • NEW YORK • SHARJAH

A CIP catalogue record for this title is available from the British Library.

ISBN 9781035871742 (Paperback)
ISBN 9781035871766 (ePub e-book)
ISBN 9781035871759 (Audiobook)

www.austinmacauley.com

First Published 2024
Austin Macauley Publishers Ltd®
1 Canada Square
Canary Wharf
London
E14 5AA

Abid Dar
Jim Butler aka Mr Thomas
Jim Sloan
Carl Cullingford

Table of Contents

Dhundhala[1] Delhi

Tuk tuk driver in Paharganj, New Delhi

Punjabi farmers far north, needing rain
Millions south breathing, red burnt grain.
It's called smog, the W.H.O. helpfully explain
Heat and dust, but don't take Ruth in vain.

Cliches for sale in the circle of naught
Bazaar over there, shoes forever taut.
Bulan's helicopter flip-flopping, unsought
Pull pity on a wire as if it's a sport.
We immerse ourselves in the calm cool fort
Or, we must spin forever in labyrinthine Connaught.

@kpmellor ©

---

[1] Dhundhala = Foggy

New Delhi Station

New Delhi Railway Station

How did he do that?
How did he know that?
He wanted platform twelve
How did he move like that?

He must be my age or more
I might have made platform four
Not a great time to delve
Into a case bigger than most
A challenge well met by my host
His looks tell me he'll not boast
Just a generous tip or you're toast

Not for the first time my train of thought
Continued from New to Old Delhi
Over and above the milling throng
Up here, along there or naught
My knees, no bags are jelly
This is your seat, rarely wrong
Yet again, a lesson in class
One not possible to surpass.

@kpmellor ©

Red Fort New Delhi

Red Fort, New Delhi

No translation required, just a nod
Holding their I-phone aloft
Always happy to oblige
With humility, not a surprise

Modi a la mode, it flowed
From faces to places, to huge spaces
India governed by laws, red and read
An oasis, a cliché, and silence rules

Despite the hum of history's stories
A simple smile in all its glories.

@kpmellor ©

Gantavy[2] Kalka

Kalka Railway Station taking 'Toy Train' to Shimla

They say all the world's in a grain
But have you been on this train

In the rain
Climbing from the plain
A city's fame
Hard to explain
Never a pain
Just catch up, with ketchup

---

[2] Gantavy = Destination

Read in the Hindustani Times

Running through
Panipat, Ambala, Pinjore to Chandigarh
One ticket, a meal never this far
Kalka next, announce the crew

Still, it rolls
Doors not closed
Breakfast gone
Chai to come, to come, to come.

@kpmellor ©

Jhilamilaata[3] Shimla

Shimla Railway Station

Idling in Kalka, temperatures dropping
Many gather by the coupling
Skill, knowledge, and strength abound
Soon start climbing, to Shimla she pounds.

Panwanoo, Solan and Kandaghat
Climbing, and straining through Kathleen's Ghat
Shoghi, Tara Devi and Summerhill
Churning past The Raj's stately ville.

How did they move the Empire here?
No thought occurred that it was queer.
In summer, thousands of people camped
Hot offices in Delhi, perhaps too cramped.

---

[3] Jhilamilaata = Shimmering

Leaving the past, into Shimla we hauled
A five-hour miracle, it's often called.

@kpmellor ©

Baadal[4] Shimla

Why zig-zag when you can zag zig?
Why no kila[5] when you can eat the view?
Working, chugging through Himalayan mist
Only the theatre adds more to the grist.
Rain, more rain, overwhelming but the few
Neem[6] bending, clouds curving, not giving a fig.

Smog long gone, overnight in the sidings
Training, not railing, through the incessant climb.
Non-stop dieseling, platforms stand agape
Stations stationary, breathing landscape.
From red to deep green, colours all chime
Into a Shimla sunset with heartfelt tidings.

@kpmellor ©

---

[4] Baadal = Cloud
[5] Kila = Castle
[6] Neem = Species of Tree

Shimla Dupatta[7]

Weaving my way diagonally
Holding the mist from my neck
Always stitching, finally
Check to see if that's a fleck?

Curving, curling, toasting
Riotous colour shouting loudly
Never more than showing proudly
Make an exception and start boasting.

Putting the gay in Gaiety, theatre calls
Wrapping in words historic halls
Tread the boards with regal ease
William and me shooting the breeze.

@kpmellor ©

---

[7] Dupatta = Shawl-like scarf

Svarga[8] Bound

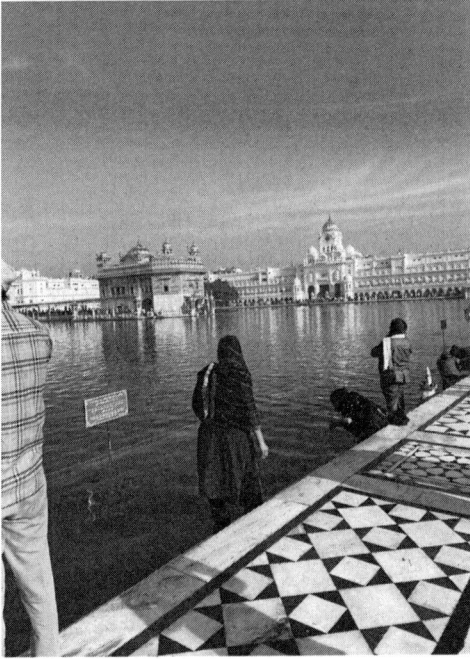

Golden Temple, Amritsar

Barrelling down the mountain tracks
Not taking sides, either will do
One hand, no hands, no confidence lacks
Wrong way, one way, anyway who knew
Living on the horn and Svarga pending
What's the real use of jaanghiya[9]?
If you have to go, a perfect ending
Trees, streams and dust; heaven is you.
No point in being straight
Just keep bending the line

---

[8] Svarga = Heaven
[9] Jaanghiya = Underclothes

Taradevi, Solan, Banasar Fort
Gone in a flick, a fleeting charm
Cars, bikes, tuk more tuk now freight
Eventually dropping out of the chine
Into Chandigarh Junction not overwrought
But… trains, seats, chai; the world is calm.

And so to sleep, perhaps I'm dreaming
Clean crisp linen is hard to beat
Chatter, chai, families all gleaming
Long hours, but still light, a golden seat
Darkness falls and landscapes are lost
Junctions, points, stations and states are crossed
Dark chaos of Amritsar, but a Golden Temple
The finest in Punjab, it's that simple

@kpmellor ©

Chandigarh
Junction *Oak and Lively*

Was it open, was it correct?
Builders building making a racket
Still chai & hulas in a packet
Station walls all charts and checks.

Three hours to wait, it's a branch
Coach 'C' a long way west
Timely boarding, be prepared lest
It's come, we've gone and I blanch

Station master all livery and duty
Make sure I board and so to sleep
Screens opposite, all voices peep
Cotton & oak, a rolling beauty.

Slow rails, dusty views, deep curtains
Service, knowledge, style and history
I doze but sleep becomes a mystery
I'll travel here again that's for certain.

@kpmellor ©

Svarn Mandir[10] Amritsar

Ranjit Singh Statue, Amritsar

No biyar[11], not here nor there
Understood; nodding in a silent groan.
Though travelling from bed to square
Overwhelmed by the glinting golden stone
No; marble not stone and pure gold.
Shoes ensconced, feet bathed and immersed
Sikh history is powerfully told
Music, words, sounds not rehearsed.
The throng shuffles forever expectant

---

[10] Svarn Mandir = Golden Temple
[11] Biyar = Beer

The epicentre agape with pure devotion
Ambrosia is more than rice repentant
Food for the Gods, overwhelming emotion.

@kpmellor ©

Jallianwala Bagh[12]

Bullet holes Jallianwala Bagh, Amritsar

The serene garden butchered by Dyer
Calm, and respectful, but no sign of fire.
Such forgiveness in the face of tragedy
What on earth did imagine he?
Against a deep dark well and also a wall
Many true citizens took their last fall.
'Shooting, rioting, insurrection all'
Dyer surely all the world should appeal.

@kpmellor ©

---

[12] JallianWala Bagh = Name of place/park

Raat Bhar Kee Bas[13]

Moving from a Partition uncut
Two roads that can only crawl
A coach station masquerading as a hut
Keep calm, carry on, never invoke a brawl

Here's your coffin, all yours for hours
Comfy exclusive and a window to boot
Dig deep, invoke some superpowers
Every man, woman, and child in high repute
Breakdowns inevitable on the commute
Waggons, cars even cycles still hoot
Surely six or thirty men can refute
But their skills are not in dispute.

Away we go, many hours through
A triangle window not to eschew
Arriving after sixteen hours the brave few
I loved every minute, who but knew?

@kpmellor ©

---

[13] Raat Bar Kee Bas = Overnight bus

How Many Gaddhe[14] in Jalandhar?

We dodged cows bigger than potholes
And potholes bigger than cows
Maharaja of Rajasthan's love child?
No, just serene beauty in the wild

I've not been chased by a snake
But I now have by a legless man
In a swirl of dust, cliches were for sale
Trained to drag pity without fail

Phones, new clothes, and curtains are Boden
Covering the triple-glazed nursery
The central reservation is home to many
Pull up a brick and settle without a bursary

Cigarette and alcohol exclusion zone
Just inside the city gates
Follow the spices to the Kulchur Club
Straight to blasted Rotten Row
Hanger left at Checkpoint Charlie
Skirt the three witches; they're on the left!

@kpmellor ©

---

[14] Gaddhe = Pit/Pothole

Jodhpur The Neela[15] City

Jodhpur (Blue City) Skyline

Happiness, nothing to prove in the streets
Dogs littering the alleys in high shrieks
High steps, higher seats, blue to the core
Press the bell and view magnificent Mehrangarh

---

[15] Neela = Blue

Winging it in the Gold Bar, smoking and mirrors
Welcomes not coming well, Kingfisher has flew
Sobriety abandoned, lights dimmed, feeling blue
History reinvented, friends uninvited, not carers

'Let's go' we mimed, the blue city turning black in colour
Winging it, Nai Sarak's dark space was a relief
Hula hoops, spiced up, blackness, just whisky teeth
Cricket, spirits, the cream of the crop, not Muller

Dogs howling, not Lassi, we know we're not barking
As for the others, the rooftops hide the smiles
Slow progress, tuking our way a night on the tiles
Juna Mahal alleys, our fears, light and candles sparking.

@kpmellor ©

Clocking On

A family man stands guard, all whirrs and cogs
Loyalty is the oil that ticks all the tocks
When a family commits to timing the clocks
A city relies on good people, not forgetting the dogs.

Leaving the tower is such sweet sorrow
Closing the gates, though too short again
One stop, halting against toast and grain
Jaipur, all pink, looms and it's tomorrow.

@kpmellor ©

Jaipur Khushiyon[16]

Amber Fort Jaipur (Pink City)

Fading light seems right
Garden at night, amber by day
No chance to enhance, windy Palace, a trance
Golden sights tinged with night.

Om gone, just as well
Claustrophobic clouds, windows to spare
Curtains enclosing a view of nowhere
A dual carriageway blazing, no wonder he fell.

---

[16] Khushiyon = Happiness

Sleeping attached to a box
Owning and living all hard knocks
Daylight creeps in through a crack
I've upgraded, it was only a sack.

Storing a beer, eating, not sleeping
Peeking at the library, all booked
Awake as I iron, I wish I'd looked
Still, another day, Jaipur only peeping

@kpmellor ©

Business In a Bucket

Growing the grains
Sowing the seeds
Squatting a corner
Hot winds howling
Could not be warmer
Not just a performer
Fill youngster's needs
To eat, everyone gains
Tossed, spun, soaked in oil
Mixed and wrapped in foil
It might not look but it is
A business in a bucket.

@kpmellor ©

Chandi Chowk a Market Miracle

Chandni Chowk, Old Delhi

Keeping up, coping sound
Sidestepping like Barry John
Overtaken with a legless bound
Moving at pace, quicker, then gone.

Offer a rupee, never a pound
A month's pay is always frowned
I might be, but they're not sad
Life is an art, it's me that's mad.

@kpmellor ©

Training Guide
West India Edition

Bags
  No bags
    Nothing, no

Coats
  Covers
    Shoes, none

West
  Passing
    Rest

Stationary, anyone?

@kpmellor ©

Delhi Drummer Girl

Traffic signals flash a life
Dodging motors not a concern
Lights red, speed read, no strife
Mum pushes a barefoot drummer
She knows the drill, time to burn
To be fair she knows to hit a beat
Despite where, when and the bare feet
B'dang b'dang trill and para trill
Those eyes, they search a western soul
What's a rupee between you and nil
Nothing; but tomorrow she will repeat
The same beat with bare feet
Mum will know how to greet
On this, the busiest Delhi street.

@kpmellor ©

Delhi Farewell

Bahrain Airport

Last days, shorter than some
Tiles, more tiles as we release
At least, at last, we can roll in the space
Delhi, goodbye; I'm more than numb.

Last look at the Labyrinth, last polish to boot
Spinning forever, I found it bizarre
Still, the powers offer me a bazar
Fond farewells Mother India, no dispute

Phasing through shining and gleaming Bahrain
Opening the headrest is such a pain
Still, to visit India will need more than a plane
I loved it so much, it is easy to explain.

@kpmellor ©

Suffolk To Norfolk
Two Peoples Apart

Switching directions from a Suffolk town
Hungry in a suit, night out long passed
Share a zoom with me, steel water to the fore
My bag is bigger than your bag and my shoulders
Glad to be either Welsh or Irish, can't say for certain
Feed my spots with loud chilli crisps
XXXL drinks bottle whilst drawing a ship
Telling the chemist how important she is
NHS, doctors, nurses, hospitals to blame, not me!

@kpmellor ©

Italy Uncovered

If you are insisting that
Rome is home, Trieste the best
If you have a momento from Sorrento
So sing sweet
As a tenor in Siena
Then Sogna Lontano

@kpmellor ©

Drain Brain

What is it worth to live a dream?
Memories are good if only seen
Once real, they collapse into the mire
Where now is pain, once was fire.

Giving all through a vortex of spin
The end asks forlornly why begin?
Was it worth the light to see the flame?
Not sure but I can feel the pain.

@kpmellor ©

Hen House

Brides bouncing, early rain
Clearest photos, all the same
Euro offie, vodie off
Politics personal, rough or not.

Birthday girls squeaking all
Yesterday's sleight the only call
Dialect, not Welsh, Dai ok
Beers, no leeks, flowing today

Rime, no rhyme, no flow
Amplitude, solitude; time to go.

@kpmellor ©

Arthur of the Square Ironing Board

Arthur Guinness. I'll drink to that.
Arthur Berry. He's more than all write.
Arthur Minute. One hundred and twenty per hour.
Arthur Mo. He'll be back later.
Arthur Askey. I thank you.
Arthur Mullard. Well 'ard.
Arthur Lowe. His Dad's in the army.
Arthur Ashe. New balls, please.
Arthur Conan Doyle. Hadn't a clue.
Arthur Garfunkel. Simon says.
Arthur Miller. Climbed a monro.
Arthur Wellesley. Gave Napoleon the boot.
Arthur Rimbaud. Illuminated.
Arthur Brown. He's on fire.
Arthur Albiston. United forever.
Arthur 'Big Boy' Crudup. His baby should never've left him.
Arthur Ode. This ain't one so good night Guinevere.

@kpmellor ©

You & Me

You crane
You see
You ain't
You are
You be
You Vlad

There's a crime 'ere

@kpmellor ©

Tamla

Marvin wasn't Gaye
Diana wasn't from Ross
Percy didn't play cricket
Aretha wasn't frank in a past life.

Four Tops fourever
Jackson Five mike not required
Stevie Wonder had his fingertips
Miracles they were

Sam couldn't cook
Isley, hey bro
Holland wasn't Dozier than Holland
Sly Stone rocked
Jackie wil some and more.

@kpmellor ©

Ian Curtis Rip

What is it worth to live a dream
Memories all gone now, rarely seen
Once real, collapsing into the mire
Where now is pain, once was fire.

Giving all through a gloom of spin
The end asking vainly, why begin?
Was it worth the highs to feel the pain?
Probably, maybe, definitely not again.

@kpmellor ©

I've Seen That House Before

A house, the house now derelict
I've seen the cracks, that light, that sky
She had legs that touched the ground
Eyes, looking, glowing, reminding of youth.
Who is it, where is it, I cannot tell
Glimpses of a town, a square, a beach?
Creating my own substation.

Why again, only Morpheus knows
Somnus lived next door I'm sure
Climbing the stairs, step by careful step
Still secure, I think but how?
She'll be there waiting for me, surely
I've seen those eyes and nearly died
Too good for me, I browsed then cried.

@kpmellor ©

Poets Remembered

Samuel Taylor Coleridge

Between 1772 and 1834
He wrote in the Lakes and his dear Exmoor
A busy poet whose unfinished lines
To the tutored eye were miraculous signs
Of Kubla Khan and Christabel
Of love, tranquillity and sleep did tell.
A vicar's son, soon to Cambridge sent
He ran away as a dragoon in Kent.
He reformed and with Wordsworth's summer salads
Is famous for the 'Lyrical Ballads'

John Donne

He was a devious deville was John Donne
Born in 1751, just gone.
One minute lewd, the next moral,
With Essex to Cadiz, he sail'd o'er coralle.
He returned to write sonnets, elegies and sermons,
Poems, prose and conceits about Germans.
Despite lively words and metaphysical calls
He lived to become the Dean of St Paul's.
Dying replete in 1632,
Or just after half past four to you.

Matthew Arnold

When Arnold was young his headmaster father
Taught him the rules of decency and morality.
But moonlight and romance put him in a lather
Hard life intruded and fought the Muse.
A poet he was and a school inspector
Of Greek legend and politics, he avoided banality.
An essayist in social mores and a collector
An academic Victorian stand if you choose.

Algernon Charles Swinburne

The ebb, flow and rage of a filling sea
Like the spirit of a rebellious figure,
Shaking dangerously the family tree,
The High Church, Kings, priests; help me pull the trigger.
A wild man to wildlife drawn,
Pre-Raphaelites the centre of the storm
He abandoned all, though his art was never worn,
His talent from Eton to eaten by 1909s dawn.

Thomas Chatterton

Had Sir Ian been a poet,
And writ with pen not his stern bat,
You'd see a man who was certainly no stoic,
But a Romantic with tousled hair, but that
Merely eighteen years at the Muse's side he sat.
At full pace in Bristol, an eighteenth-century beatnik
To London, he moved, peaked and died of arsenic.

William Blake

Innocence:

Merry, merry Soho
Artists here and there,
A keen engraver's lad
Taken to Christian life,
Took an artist as a wife,
Saw visions but was not mad.

Experience:

Deep binding and cutting strife,
Keenly monogamous all-seeing wife,
Frightening visions of a country dying,
Pitiful, darkening; Satan only crying.

@kpmellor ©

Dunes

Whether I am here or never
Weathered marram bends the air
Warming ears with a deafening noise
The senses are not defeated.
Sands shifting with sea holly
They always move with thyme
Vipers, primrose, vetch and harrow
Blow away any sense of sorrow
Whistling without sense of time
Grain-pulling and pushing melancholy
Not a second is one howl cheated
Against the gales, there is no poise
Looking to sea, but not to stare
A father, a sailor, may live forever.

@kpmellor ©